Police Horses

by Katie Clark

Consultant:
Bonnie V. Beaver
College of Veterinary Medicine
Texas A&M University

BEARPORT
PUBLISHING

New York, New York

Credits

Cover and Title Page, © Jose Gil/Shutterstock; 4–5, © Richard B. Levine/Newscom; 6–7, © Andrew Sole/Alamy; 8–9, © Sharon Morris/Shutterstock; 10–11, © Jorg Hackemann/Shutterstock; 12–13, © Mike Maple/ZUMApress/Newscom; 14–15, © justasc/Shutterstock; 16–17, © Alina Solovyova-Vincent/iStockphoto; 18–19, © Alexey Stiop/Shutterstock; 20–21, © Kim Karpeles/Alamy; 22T, 22B, © iStockphoto/Thinkstock; 22C, © justasc/Shutterstock; 23T, © Jorg Hackemann/Shutterstock; 23C, © Bucchi Francesco/Shutterstock; 23B, © Alina Solovyova-Vincent/iStockphoto.

Publisher: Kenn Goin
Creative Director: Spencer Brinker
Design: Becky Daum
Photo Researcher: Arnold Ringstad

Library of Congress Cataloging-in-Publication Data

Clark, Katie, 1962-
  Police horses / by Katie Clark.
      p. cm. — (We work!: Animals with jobs)
  Includes bibliographical references and index.
  ISBN-13: 978-1-61772-896-9 (library binding) — ISBN-10: 1-61772-896-9 (library binding)
  1. Police horses—Juvenile literature. 2. Mounted police—Juvenile literature. I. Title.
  HV7957.C53 2014
  636.1—dc23
                                   2013011509

For more information, write to Bearport Publishing Company, Inc., 45 West 21st Street, Suite 3B, New York, New York 10010. Printed in the United States of America.

10 9 8 7 6 5 4 3 2 1

Contents

A Police Horse Named Buster

Buster raced through a crowded city.

He was chasing a thief.

The police officer riding Buster used **reins** to guide him.

Within minutes, Buster reached the thief and the officer **arrested** him.

Buster the police horse

5

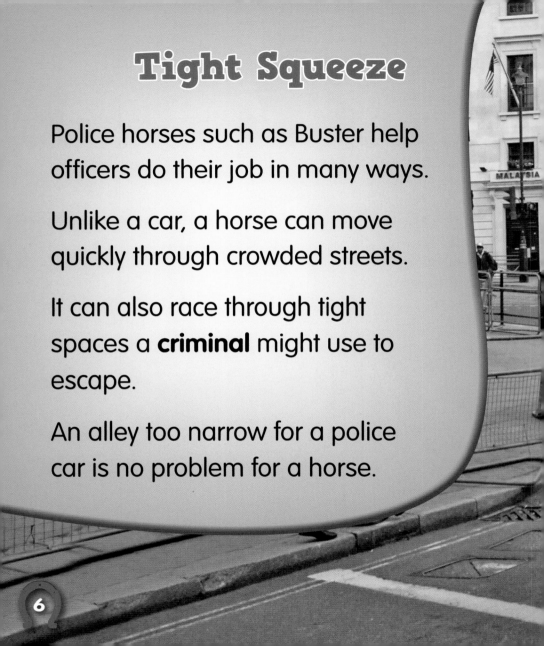

Tight Squeeze

Police horses such as Buster help officers do their job in many ways.

Unlike a car, a horse can move quickly through crowded streets.

It can also race through tight spaces a **criminal** might use to escape.

An alley too narrow for a police car is no problem for a horse.

Racing to the Crime

Police horses help stop criminals because they run faster than people.

In 2005, a Florida officer got a call that someone was robbing a nearby bank.

The officer raced to the bank on his police horse.

When the robber saw the horse, he gave up.

He knew he could not outrun the horse!

a police horse
guarding a bank

Big and Tall

To do their jobs, police horses have to be really big.

Most weigh more than 1,000 pounds (454 kg).

They stand more than five feet (1.5 m) tall.

A horse's height lets the officer on its back see over people's heads.

This makes it easy for the officer to quickly spot trouble in a crowd.

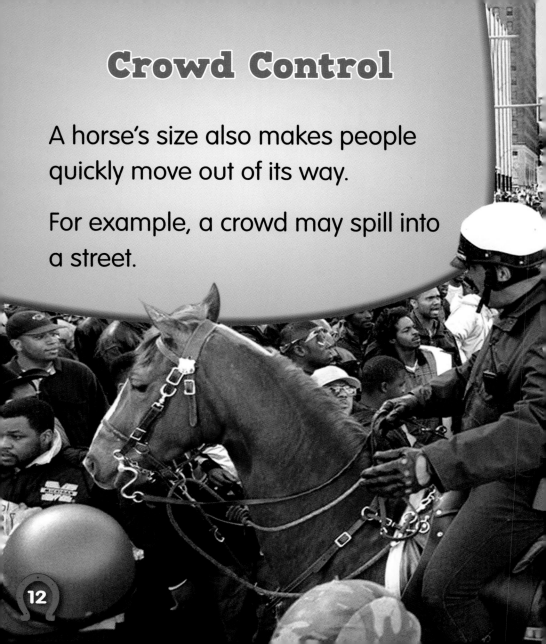

Crowd Control

A horse's size also makes people quickly move out of its way.

For example, a crowd may spill into a street.

12

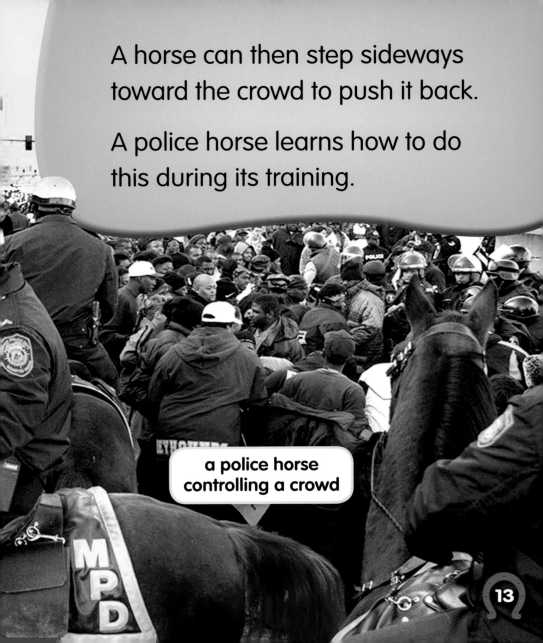

A horse can then step sideways toward the crowd to push it back.

A police horse learns how to do this during its training.

a police horse controlling a crowd

13

In Training

A horse is usually trained for three to six months to do police work.

During that time, the horse and its police partner learn to work together.

The horse learns to follow the officer's **commands**.

The horse also learns to stay calm around loud noises, such as sirens.

Joining the Force

To join the police, a horse usually must be at least two years old.

It must be large and gentle, too.

A horse must also pass a health checkup by a **veterinarian**.

a veterinarian checking a horse

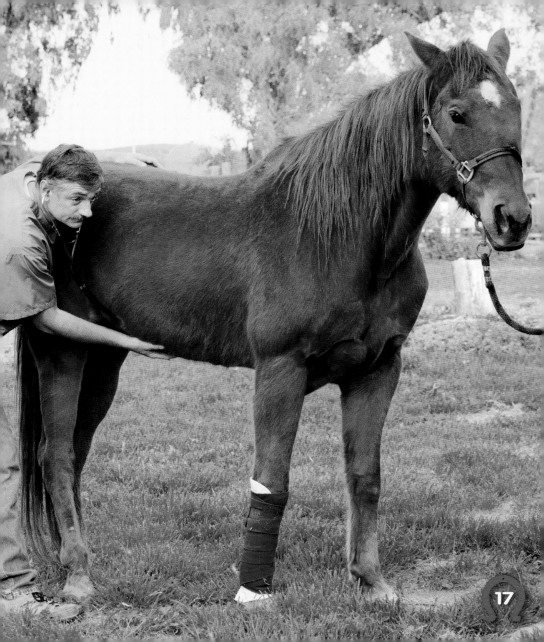

At Home on the Police Force

Most police horses live in **stables** near the police station.

Others stay on farms near town.

When horses are not working, they can run and play.

They eat grain, hay, and grass.

The Best Job

Police horses are not always fighting crime.

One of their best jobs is visiting schools.

Students get to meet the horses and talk to the officers.

The students even get to pet the horses, which they love to do.

After all, police horses are a lot more fun to pet than police cars!

Glossary

arrested (uh-REST-id) stopped and held someone for breaking the law

commands (kuh-MANDZ) orders given by someone to do something

criminal (KRIM-uh-nuhl) a person who has broken the law

reins (RAYNZ) straps used to control or guide a horse

stables (STAY-buhlz) buildings in which horses are kept

veterinarian (*vet*-ur-uh-NER-ee-uhn) a doctor who cares for animals

23

Index

Read More

Apte, Sunita. *Police Horses (Horse Power).* New York: Bearport (2007).

Nagle, Jeanne. *Working Horses (Horsing Around).* New York: Gareth Stevens (2011).

Owen, Ruth. *Horses (The World's Smartest Animals).* New York: Rosen (2012).

Learn More Online

To learn more about police horses, visit
www.bearportpublishing.com/WeWork

About the Author

Katie Clark has written many books, articles, and apps for children.
She enjoys spending time reading, writing, and playing make-believe
with her daughters.